Planets in Our Solar System

MERCURY

by Jody S. Rake

Pebble Explore is published by Pebble, an imprint of Capstone,
1710 Roe Crest Drive
North Mankato, Minnesota 56003
www.capstonepub.com

**Library of Congress Cataloging-in-Publication Data is available on the
Library of Congress website.**

ISBN: 978-1-9771-2391-6 (hardcover)
ISBN: 978-1-9771-2691-7 (paperback)
ISBN: 978-1-9771-2428-9 (eBook PDF)

Summary: The smallest planet in our solar system is also the closest to the
sun. That means on Mercury, one year is just 88 days long! Discover more
facts about the small but mighty Mercury.

Image Credits:
Getty Images: Science & Society Picture Library, 8; iStockphoto:
Pomogayev, 10; NASA: JHUAPL/Carnegie Institution of Washington/ DLR/
Smithsonian Institution, 16, JHUAPL/NASA/Bill Ingalls, 28, Johns Hopkins
University Applied Physics Laboratory/Carnegie Institution of Washington,
15, 17, 18; Science Source: David A. Hardy, 12–13, Detlev van Ravenswaay,
21, ESA/Christophe Carreau, 22–23, Frank Zullo, 5, Justin Kelly/Stocktrek
Images, 20, TIM BROWN, 26–27; Shutterstock: AF studio, 4, delcarmat, 11,
Dotted Yeti, Cover left, 1, Macrovector, 6–7, Mopic, 19, Naeblys, Back Cover,
NASA images, Cover, Oleg Golovnev, 9, Vadim Sadovski, 14, Withan Tor, 25

Design Elements:
Shutterstock: Arcady, BLACKDAY, ebes, LynxVector, phipatbig, Stefan
Holm, veronchick_84

Editor: Alison Deering; Designer: Jennifer Bergstrom; Media Researcher:
Tracy Cummins; Production Specialist: Tori Abraham

Table of Contents

Words in **bold** are in the glossary.

The Sun's Nearest Neighbor

A tiny white dot appears in the night sky. It looks like a star that is far away. But it is not a star. It is a planet. It is Mercury.

Mercury is the closest planet to the sun. It has no moons of its own.

Mercury is the fastest planet. It moves around the sun very quickly.

Imagine a plane could fly as fast as Mercury moves. It would circle Earth four times in one hour!

Mercury

Mercury is the smallest planet. It is much closer to the sun than Earth is.

From Mercury, the sun would look three times larger. The sunlight would be seven times brighter. It would feel much hotter.

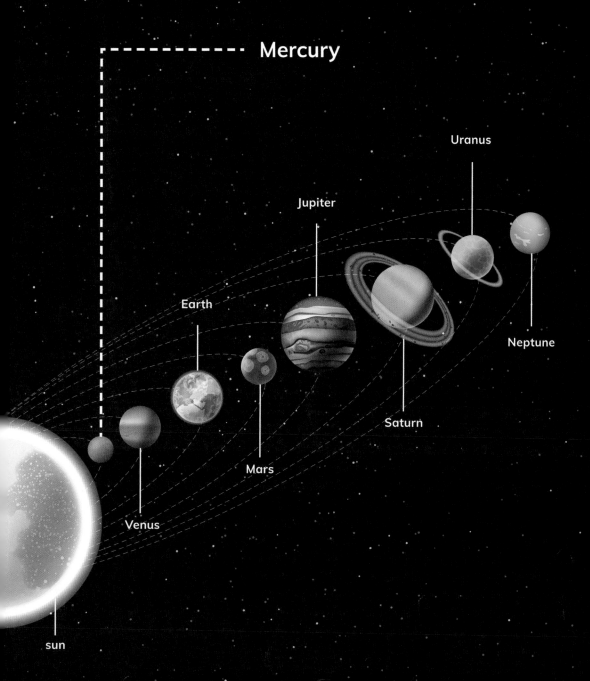

Mercury

Uranus

Jupiter

Earth

Neptune

Mars

Saturn

Venus

sun

Speedy Mercury

No one knows when Mercury was discovered. Thousands of years ago, people knew it was a planet. They knew this because it didn't twinkle like a star.

More than 400 years ago, a **scientist** saw Mercury for the first time. His name was Galileo. He used a tool called a **telescope**.

Scientists study the sky with a telescope.

Mercury is named for the Roman god Mercury. He had wings on his heels. They made him the fastest of all the gods.

Mercury is the fastest planet. It was named after this speedy god.

The Roman god Mercury

Mercury moves around the sun. The way it moves is called an **orbit**. It does not move in a round circle. Its path is shaped more like an egg.

The sun is not in the middle of Mercury's path. Some days, it is close to the sun. Other days, it is far away.

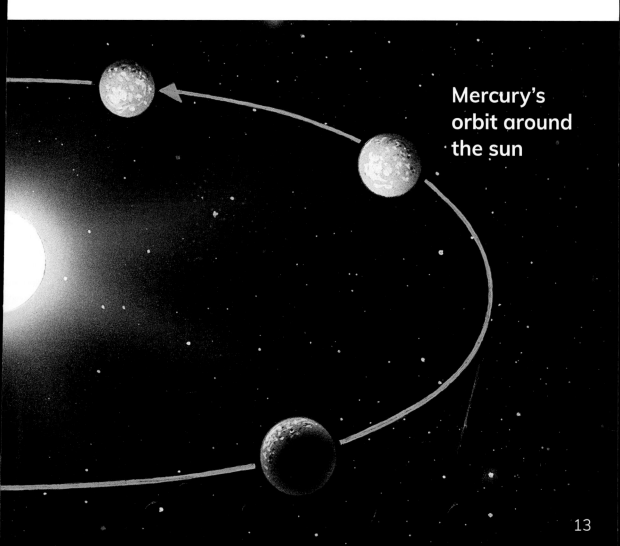

Mercury's orbit around the sun

A Rocky Planet

Mercury is a rocky planet. It is covered with large holes. These holes are called **craters**.

They were formed by space rocks. These rocks are called **meteors.** They hit Mercury long ago.

Meteors in space

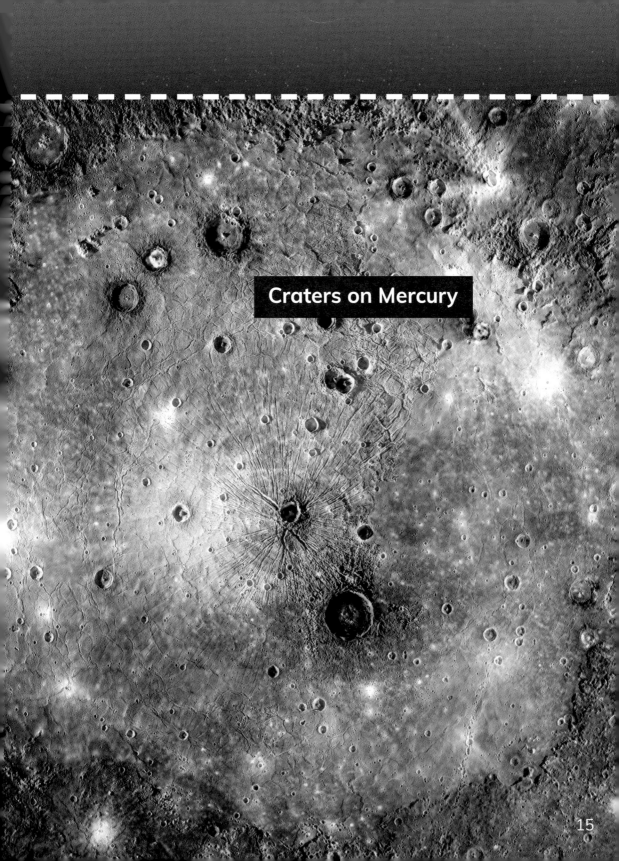

Craters on Mercury

Mercury may have **quakes**. These shake the ground. The movement makes mountains and valleys.

One of these valleys is called the Great Valley. It is larger than the Grand Canyon.

Mercury also has **volcanoes**. Some people believe they are old. They are probably not active.

Mercury's Great Valley

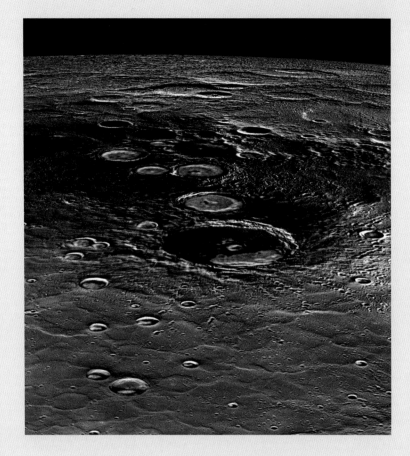

Frozen water on Mercury

Mercury may have frozen water.
It would be found in deep holes.
The holes are at the very top and
bottom of the planet.

Hot and Cold

Mercury is the second-hottest planet. There is a band of **gas** that covers the planet. It holds heat from the sun close. Even when the sun is up, the sky still looks black.

Heat from the sun warms Mercury quickly. The days are very hot. When the sun sets, it cools quickly.

Mercury's surface

sun

Mercury

The sun is very strong. It makes a wind that can reach planets. This is called solar wind.

The sun is very hot and very strong.

Solar wind hits Mercury.

Mercury is blasted by this wind. It
may wear away rocks on the planet.

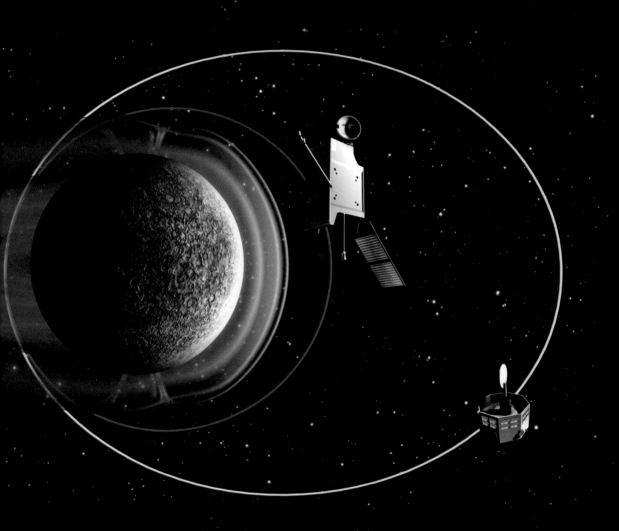

Two spacecraft circle Mercury.

People have not been to Mercury. But we have sent **spacecraft** to explore it.

The first ship flew past Mercury more than 40 years ago. It got a good view. It took many pictures.

The second ship circled Mercury from 2011 to 2015. It helped us learn even more about the planet.

The third ship left Earth in October 2018. It will start circling Mercury in December 2025.

Short Years and Long Days

Mercury has very long days. But its years are very short. One year there is about three months on Earth.

If you lived on Mercury, you would have a birthday every three months! That is how long it takes Mercury to circle the sun.

Mercury moves around the sun quickly. But it spins very slowly. People used to think it didn't spin at all.

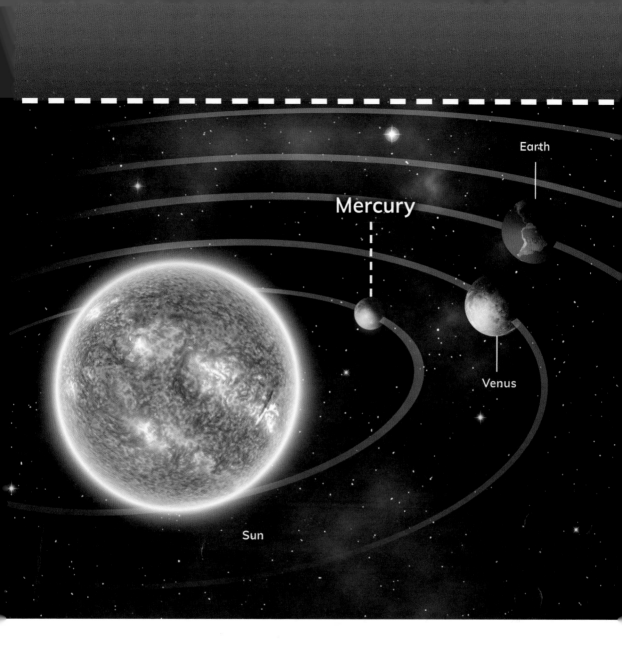

Earth

Mercury

Venus

Sun

Earth makes one full spin per day.
It takes almost two months on Earth
for Mercury to spin around one time.

Mercury has no air or water.

Gravity is what keeps us on the ground. Smaller planets have less of this. Mercury's gravity is less than half of Earth's.

There is no life on Mercury. It gets
way too hot during the day. At night it
gets much too cold. There is no air to
breathe. There is no water to drink.

When to See Mercury

Mercury can only be seen from Earth at certain times. The best time is an hour before sunrise. You can also see it an hour after sunset.

Sometimes Mercury moves across the sun. From Earth, it looks like a tiny dark spot. You must use a special telescope to see it.

The next time this happens won't be until November 13, 2032.

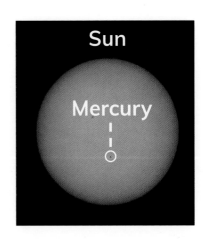

Fast Facts

Name:
Mercury

Location:
closest planet to the sun

Planet Type:
rocky

Discovered:
unknown; first seen through telescope
in 1600s

Moons:

Glossary

crater (KRAY-tur)—a large hole in the ground caused by crashing rocks

gas (GASS)—something that is not solid or liquid and does not have a definite shape

gravity (GRAV-uh-tee)—a force that pulls objects together

meteor (MEE-tee-ur)—a piece of rock that burns up as it passes through a planet's atmosphere

orbit (OR-bit)—to travel around an object in space; also the path an object follows while circling an object in space

quake (kwayk)—a very strong shaking or trembling of the ground

scientist (SYE-uhn-tist)—a person who studies the world around us

spacecraft (SPAYSS-kraft)—a vehicle for travel beyond Earth's atmosphere

telescope (TEL-uh-skohp)—a tool people use to look at objects in space; telescopes make objects in space look closer than they really are

volcano (vol-KAY-noh)—an opening in a planet's surface that sometimes sends out hot lava, steam, and ash

Read More

Baines, Becky. *Planets*. Washington, D.C.: National Geographic Kids, 2016.

Bloom, J.P. *Mercury*. North Mankato, MN: Capstone Classroom, 2017.

Sommer, Nathan. *Mercury*. Minneapolis: Bellwether Media, 2019.

Internet Sites

European Space Agency Kids
https://www.esa.int/kids/en/learn/Our_Universe/Planets_and_moons/Mercury

NASA Science: Solar System Exploration
https://solarsystem.nasa.gov/planets/mercury/overview/

National Geographic
https://www.nationalgeographic.com/science/space/solar-system/mercury/

Index